I0603592

for life

poetry

by Emma Briggs

Copyright © 2020 by Emma Briggs

"for life"

All rights reserved. No part of this book may be reproduced or distributed
without the express written permission of the author.
ISBN: 978-0-646-81545-9

Cover design and illustrations by Iris Maertens www.irisistible.design

www.facebook.com/emmajbriggs

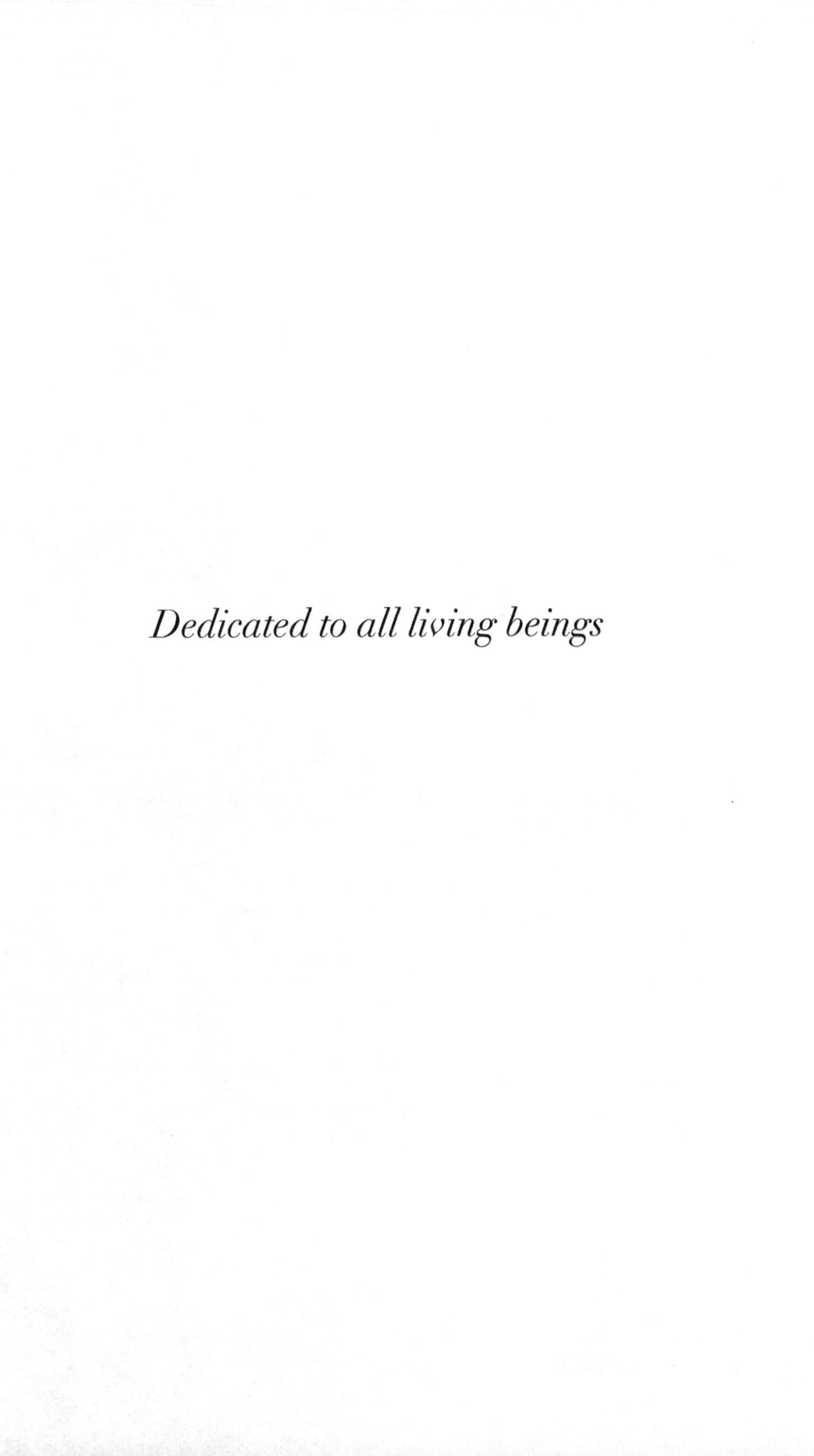

Dedicated to all living beings

contents

forward

A good friend of mine has always claimed that she hated poetry. To me it sounded like an impossible generalisation, but I was pretty sure she wasn't alone in her inexplicable disgust for the rhythmic composition of words. In fact, I'd assumed that it was an almost universal inclination.

To say that I enjoy writing poetry is not exactly accurate. It's more like a compulsion which I try to keep under control. In my teens and twenties I was unable to stop myself from composing poems, often several a day. It was therapy rather than literature.

When I decided I wanted to be a proper writer, I knew that I would have to move over into the prose field. Nobody was interested in poetry, and in the unlikely event that there was going to be any money to be earned through words, I was certain it would have to be in novels.

I tried. It was not easy for me because I have the unusual problem of being too concise. I have to force myself to insert extra words around the few which I consider necessary. With some effort, I expanded into blogs, short stories, and eventually managed a full-length novel or two.

It has been a struggle building an audience and none of my writing has made much of an impact until someone asked if I'd ever tried poetry. My secret habit had been suppressed for about a decade and it had never occurred to me that

other people would have any interest in reading verse, par-
ticularly my verse.

It turned out I was wrong. When I decided I had nothing to
lose and posted my first poem online, a surprising number
of strangers reacted positively. I wrote many more and re-
hashed some of my old ones and readers actually respond-
ed, engaged and started following my account. *"Who'd have
thought?"* as my poetry-hating friend remarked.

I would like to think that it is because aesthetically pleasing,
structured words are what a growing number of readers
need at this point in history. Our current existence is full of
mess and ugliness. In the face of this discord, we can try to
expose the brutal facts in essays or to distract ourselves
with fantasy stories, but there are many who find these
words difficult to swallow.

Sometimes when words are shaped into an elegant spear of
truth, it can be enough to pierce a shielded heart. When
our hearts are opened, we have no choice but to confront
reality as it is, and this is what makes poetry important in
our lives.

fear for life

Sweat

Heat, humidity, the saltwater slick of our skin:
this is what we must get used to.
We try to stop the temperature rising
but I fear it's too late
and that sweat is the least of our worries.
More cyclones, fires, wars:
I can't even think about it.
What will they say, your children
(not mine, they don't exist)
when they learn how it used to be,
how we knew what was to come
and failed to stop it?
We could have stopped it.
Once it seemed as if we might.
Now I fear it's too late
and our fate
is sealed beneath this saltwater slick.

Sick

I'm sick, the Earth is sick, we want to stay in bed.
Bring us soup.
Our systems aren't working as they should.
We're running a temperature.
There's a virus inside us
infecting our vitality, sucking our strength.
Our cells repel it but we're tired.
For me it's been a day or two and
I know I'll recover soon.
It's been decades for the planet and
the prognosis isn't good.
This virus is particular.
It knows if it kills the host that will be the end.
It must mutate for its own sake
but can it ever happen?
A thick fog compresses my brain.
A blanket of gas suffocates my world.
We struggle to clear the air,
to fight the fever,
to breathe.

Blame

I wonder what they think about,
those coal barons, those oil tycoons and
their political puppets,
when they think about the future
and the lives their kids will lead?

Do they think that their money
can somehow save them from the weather?
Do they think the scientists are lying?
Do they think they can move to Mars?
Do they think? Do they care?

It's very hard for me to see
how someone can be smart enough
to gather so much wealth and power,
and still not understand
the outcomes of their actions.

When the world heats over,
when the storms increase
with the fires, floods and droughts,
when the ice melts and the waters rise,
will they be surprised?

Will they try to shift the blame?
Will they claim they didn't know?
Maybe they will feel ashamed,
apologise and make amends, or
deny, deny until they die

Cycle of Lies

When oil company executives,
and corrupt politicians
give millions to 'think tanks',
founded by bankers,
captains of industry
and emperors of media,
to fund 'academics'
to research deceitfully
to deny climate science,
to protect vested interests,
to be held up as proof
by the media it came from,
to be swallowed as truth
by dissatisfied masses
nostalgic for a resource boom
which won't happen again,
who use it to justify
voting for the parties
who paid for the lies,
as glaciers are melting,
as species are dying,
as we're running out of time,
then we're fucked.

Suicide Parade

I ran across a bridge in a dream
faster than I ever could awake.
There was a parade.
We were going to stop it.
The marching band stomped to the beat,
never knowing where the music led.
We observed they were headed
over the edge.
They couldn't see it.
They marched in their sleep.
The only way to save the day
was to divert the leader,
to change their fatal course
even if it upset the order,
even if it caused discord,
even if the tune was ruined,
at least we'd all be safe.
I woke up before the band did,
so I don't know how the story ends.
Will we ever stop the parade?
Will we avert disaster?
Or will sleep-walking musicians
trample across our bodies,
determined to keep the rhythm,
to obey the leader,
to advance over the side of the bridge,
to march us to our death.

City Life

In the grey city
(doesn't matter which one),
they fight the cold concrete
with art and bars and fashion,
street trees and flower boxes,
and on sunny days
when people come alive,
bringing paint and speakers,
sometimes it works.

On other days the heavy clouds
mute the colours,
the thick cement
drowns the music,
the funnelled wind
drains the blood
and life retreats
to drink in the basement.

Fear

Some people are afraid of men with bombs,
whom the papers pretend
populate these streets,
although they don't.

Some are frightened of leaky boats
full of persecuted people,
risking death for life;
they aren't the threat.

Some are alarmed by the pace of change,
but work and words will always shift
and new ways to see the world
are as inevitable as time.

Some of us are scared of the greed and corruption
in our leaders and media,
which could condemn us all,
unless we resist.

Some of us dread what is physically happening,
every second all over the planet,
the chemistry experiment we conduct with air
on the biology of everything.

Terror only helps when the danger is real
and if it results in action.
Could the power of fear finally move us to try
to preserve life on Earth?

Idiocy

I try and write about something else
but it's all I can think about
sometimes.
It's just
the sheer idiocy of the situation.
We have this problem, this huge problem,
this problem which threatens each and every being
living in our world,
and we have the solution, the answer right there
where it has been for decades
and yet
some people, many people, people with power
shut their eyes, block their ears,
run around blindly, shouting lies,
and deliberately derail the train to our salvation.
It's suicide,
also homicide and genocide and ecocide.
What's wrong with these people?

Hungry

So when someone says, *fuck it,*
I'm going to vote for Duterte, Bolsonaro or Trump,
are they giving up on life?
Are they saying, *"Bring it all on.*
Let's fight to the end.
I'm not gonna win, so everyone can suffer.
I'll tear you apart.
I don't care any more."
Did their mothers not love them,
all these insecure people,
or did society let them down?
How are they entranced
by the hungry monsters,
those narcissistic enough to reach the top
without a vision?
Their power depends on desperate people.
When there's enough to eat,
enough to share,
when life is not a constant battle,
the monsters have nothing to offer.
This lesson from history is very clear,
so when will we learn it?

Syria

Plastic bags empty of U.N. aid,
filled with corpses of children instead,
placed in rows amongst colourless rubble.
Parents howl.
Shells explode.
The drones are silent.
Death in every direction and nowhere to run.
While the tribes kill each other
for history, resources or god,
identical grey bodies
don't remember.

Imagine

Can you imagine when your city explodes?
Will you stick around in the rubble?
Pick a side and fight to death for your life
or scavenge and hide to survive.
You can run through the desert,
and climb up the mountains,
find a boat and cross the sea,
or try to fly without a visa.
Which will your best option be?
To be shot, to starve, to freeze or to drown:
which is the best way to die?
And if you make it to the other side,
the battle's just begun.
Now you must fight to survive with words,
with documents and time.
In a tent through winter, on an island for years,
how will you rebuild your dreams
so far from home and all that you know
and whoever is left in your family?
Can you imagine when your only hope
lies in our humanity?

Stuck

Been here for six years,
nothing to do, nowhere to go,
so far from anyone I've loved,
so far from hope.

Bullets fly at home,
the rest of the world fears me,
while here the men despair
and suicide.

At night I dream of my mother,
of a time before the war.
I fly away from the island
and I am free,

until I wake to see
the grim eyes of my brothers,
fists clutching to survive
one more day.

How much longer will I stay?
How much longer can I live?
For how much longer can you
ignore me?

The old lady and the boy

This nation is a thoughtless and mean
adolescent chasing relevance,
knocking down his grandmother,
stomping over a country
as ancient as dreaming, older than time.

While rains and rivers turned mountains into valleys,
trees and crocodiles, wallabies and humans,
grew, reproduced and died
in her deserts and forests,
and on her plains and shores.

Life ebbed and flowed
in gentle waves
around the millennia,
through seasons and cycles,
fires and floods,
until Australia was born
and everything changed.

Adam and Eve were thrown out of Eden,
the people torn apart from the land
in a brutal and sudden divorce.
Trees were chopped down, crocodiles shot,
new creatures and diseases arrived.

The waves of life
turned into spikes,
jagged peaks on a chart
in pursuit of perpetual growth,
the impossible dream.
Now the teenager rages.
He wants to be bigger and better than the rest.
He refuses to accept the limits,
but it is the old woman who makes the rules.
She knows the way things work,
every action has a reaction and in the end
balance must be restored.

Fear of Wasting Time

Not creating a thing;
not lifting anyone's mood;
not improving the view;
not planting a single seed;
not keeping something alive;
not helping anybody live;
not making anything better;
not fixing what is broken;
not changing the system:
these are the monsters
that wake me up at 3 am
and keep sleep away 'til dawn.

They terrify my night,
looming above,
filling the room,
suffocating until
the light of the sun
eventually comes
to send them out the window.

In the daytime I remember
that I might not be strong enough
now, or maybe ever,
to defeat all the monsters,
but I can kill one or two.
I can keep trying,
some days in small ways,
other days more,
to invest my time
wisely

for inner life

Part-time love

I love you, my Earth, but it hurts
too much and sometimes what I need
to get through the day is to
shut my eyes to your pain.

When I'm feeling strong I know
I'd do anything to defend you,
debate a climate denier or
climb a smokestack in the rain,

but there are times when I can't even read
the headlines or open my emails.
How can I handle the truth
while I fight to stay sane?

My love is real, but I have to concede,
partial fidelity is all I can do.

Overwhelm

too much truth hurts my brain
some bits gotta be shut out
docos leave me shaking
I wanna watch a rom-com
they need me at two meetings
I hafta pick which one
we need more people on our side
but no-one seems to care
my battery is always low
I cannot act on all I know
although my conscience screams
I must choose one thing to do
or maybe two at most
but how to decide where to spend time
when every fight is vital
is messing with my mind

Termites

Termites eat my sleep,
devour my dreams,
chew through my stability,
nibble away the foundations
of my future.

At night I hear them.
Crick, crick. So soft
it could be the winding tick
of my thoughts.

Tiny white insects
crawl deep inside,
steal my strength,
leave me hollow,
a paper facade.

Will the rain dissolve me?
Will I crumble in the wind?
I'm paralysed,
afraid to move,
perfect on the outside,
rotten within.

Tunes of Torment and Temptation

sad songs trap me here
i can't get away
i want to rise, to do something, anything
but those minor chords
tie me down
cutting as i resist
the desperate voice
clear as a funeral bell
notes so slow they sink,
seep into my skin
seduce me to let
lyrics fill my lungs
i can't breathe
i'm falling under
the fatal allure of misery

Missing

Something is missing tonight,
in a hole made darker by the light
of the rising moon.
This evening she is complete,
casting shadows on this wanting world,
heedless in her monthly glory.
Something slipped and fell down a crack where
her radiance cannot reach and
now I fear it's lost.
I can't remember what it was
though the absence howls through me
into outer space.
My mind is clouded and my body consumed
with a dull ache for whatever it is
that has gone.
Insistent lunar forces tug for attention;
if I can't see it in the moonlight
it will have to wait.
My search will begin on another night
when the shade returns to the moon,
when gravity is back.
Meanwhile I'll survive until sunrise,
exposed under her consummate glow,
incomplete.

Screens

A plover calls at night, clear and determined
to be heard,
reminding me that life is happening beyond these walls
away from these screens.
I am tired of the politicians and the hosts
so I slide through the glass door into real time
where the breeze is cool and,
though faded by a single street light,
the stars are scattered across the sky.
Leaves rustle, crickets sing and far away
the ocean breathes deeply as if it's asleep.
Something sweet summons insects on the wind.
All the people are closed in their walls
and soon the scene is also not enough for me.
I shiver a little as my restless mind
wonders what I might be missing
in the screens.

Inside again I find
I'm not able to watch the hosts,
and too sober to stand the comments.
I wish I was with friends, sitting around a fire,
watching flames until I grew tired enough
to sleep.

Current Events

I'm tired
swimming against the tide,
leaping upstream.
It would be so easy to drift along
towards the tempestuous sea,
knowing my time may be done
before I reach the maelstrom
but I can't seem to quit
resisting it,
that almost inevitable
flow to oblivion.

Imaginary Wood

She groped in the darkness
and felt cobwebs wrap her fingers
in sticky silk
but it didn't matter.
Though the rock over her head
dripped eternal drips
and the air was
rancid with rats,
in her heart a blazing fire
burned, pushing her along.
The flames licked her throat,
warming it against the damp.
Things crawled over her feet
with tiny piercing claws
and scratched a repulsive retreat
down the terrible tunnel.
She knew the fire was fuelled
with imaginary wood
which would,
one day,
inevitably turn to ash,
but it was all she had.

The War Inside

It's complicated, but is it really?
It's at least as old as love.
It's a force so strong that
when I fight against it,
the skin peels off my hands,
food tastes empty and
I lie awake each night
with the palpitating heart
of moral agony.
My brain knows that
we would never work,
not in a million years.
The nightmare that would descend
if I don't resist the force
could not be endured.
Yet how can I defy the
insistence of your skin
when our arms touch,
my chest convulses and
there's suddenly not enough oxygen
anywhere?
How can I shield myself
against those laser eyes
searing my mind
with lies I don't want to believe?
In the battle between
logic and chemistry
there will be no winners
and I will be the first casualty.

Perfect

Perfect may be a noun or a verb,
but it can never be attained.
Perfect can be a goal or a gaol.
Perfect can motivate, perfect can enslave
or perfect can paralyse.

There will always be a stain on your record,
a flaw in your beauty,
a crack in your logic,
a flea in your coat,
or a ball of dust hiding under your couch.

Admit it, expose it, accept it.
You can extract the flea and sweep the dust,
but know they will return,
so embrace the eternal struggle
or release it.

Perféct is a process without an end.
Pérfect is a concept which isn't real.
Chase it if you must, but it is only a word.

If perfect were possible, everyone would be the same,
the world would be flat,
the view would be monotone,
so enjoy your divergence,
climb up the hills and roll down the valleys
and love all the colours of life.

I wish

I wish I could say to you, *be happy,*
and you would suddenly see
you don't need to torture yourself
on that invisible rack,
but I know it doesn't work like that.

I wish I could let you know
that you can choose which thoughts
you let in, which to question
and which to evict,
but I know you wouldn't listen.

I wish you could love yourself
as much as we all do,
forgive your mistakes and mine,
be kind to your heart,
but I know you can't.

I wish you could ask for assistance,
reach out to science,
open your eyes to search for the light.
I know I don't have the answer,
but somebody else might.

It'll be okay.

Be happy, my love,
you have earned it
after striving for so many years,
after work, work, work without rest,
after shooting the troubles,
after risking it all,
after disappointment and victory,
you deserve to be free
from the pain and worry
but I hope it's with me.
We can find our way
to the garden of peace,
I promise.
We can be together
in tranquility,
I'm certain.
Just give me the word
when you're ready.

In the morning

My coffee cup is empty.
The blood pumps a little faster,
neurones spark across my brain,
as I try to forget disturbing dreams,
the dark manacle of sleep
that held me to my pillow
a few moments earlier.
It's a new day.
It may be grey, windy, damp,
but there is always promise
when birds call at dawn.
This could be the one to turn it around,
you never know.
I remind myself that whether or not
I find what I want,
I have much more than I need.
My life is a treasure, a marvel, a prize.
What a trip it's been so far!
Though the sun may be hidden by clouds,
its light slightly dimmed,
it never fails to climb the sky
each morning to reveal again
I still have a way to go.

Simple

We make life more complicated
than it's supposed to be.
Our needs are simple but our wants are vast,
convoluted, capricious
and rarely satisfied.
Who should we listen to?
Learning *what* and *how* does not take long.
It's *why* which may take a lifetime
and still remain unanswered.
Maybe there's nothing to know.
Maybe food and shelter's enough
with air to breathe
and love.

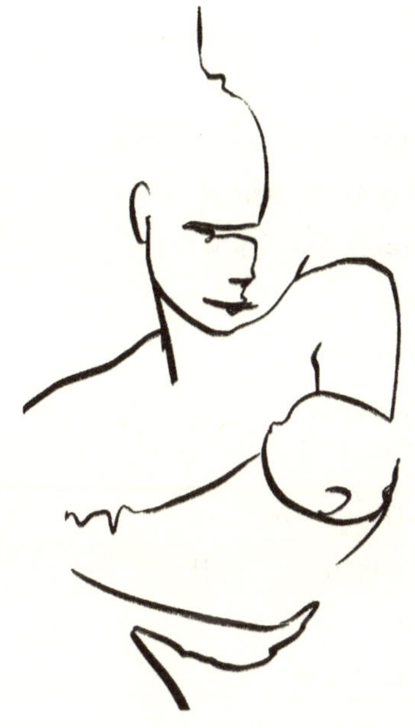

for human life

The Horror

What is there to say to horror?
The heart of darkness hides my words
but I will dive deep in a sea of tears
to rip them from the mud.

As children march in hope for tomorrow,
a soul of hate sprays blood on the walls.
His thoughts have twisted so far away
that he believes it is his right
to steal lives, to smash families,
to shatter the quiet,
to construct a terror
too sharp to ever forget.

He does not have this right.
I hope one day, alone in his cell,
his thoughts will untwist until he can see
the suffering he's unleashed.
I hope his remaining years will fill
with a torment of regret.

I hope someday, somehow we can
stop the violent cycle.
I hope, but I don't know how to forgive
this magnitude of evil.

Cold

A man froze to death on the street last night
in Australia.
How could we let this happen?
He wasn't drunk, on drugs or sick
(although that wouldn't excuse it).
He was just cold and had no home.
He'd lost his job and had no family.
Why didn't we give him a bed?
Or a blanket?
Why didn't we allow him a tent and a fire?
Why did we let him die?
The world is upside down.
The laws are back to front.
We've lost our way.
In this century there is no reason
for someone to starve or freeze,
to be locked away unjustly.
Things need to change.
We need to resist
the forces dragging us back.
We need to evolve
before it's too late.
We need to make it warm.

Remember Jemel

Another horror unfolds in the waking nightmare we call
news:
a man risks his life to disable a shooter,
chasing him, pinning him down until police arrive at the
club,
but when they do,
they do not thank the man for his bravery,
they do not hear the crowd shout, *'He saved us!'*,
they do not see *'Security'* written on his cap.
No. They shoot him
dead,
because he is black.

I sit in the spring sun on the other side of the world
and wonder why I have to read this.
Why do I inflict myself with these daily stories
of stupid hate and pointless pain?
I can't make it end,
but I can't turn away (not every time).
One day the futile, tragic news could include my name,
so I suppose I should read every word.
The least I can do is witness and care,
never stop caring,
because when the caring stops,
humanity
is lost.

Politics

From far away I hear the news
and try not to despair.
It seems the selfish side is winning
but the truth is not so simple.
I tell myself the way it goes,
that history is a cycle.
It does not progress from bad to good
but spirals and expands.
Human experience will fill
a ever-growing circle.
Each day we learn a little more
than we knew yesterday.
Highs and lows will rise and fall
and we will push the limits.
One day wisdom will prevail,
the next may be disaster.
All we can do for the love of life
is to keep the pedals turning.
We who see can try to steer it
in the best direction.
There will always be those
who push against,
and those who hold us back.
It'll work for a while
but they'll never contain
our expanding consciousness.

The War of the Comments Section

The outraged keyboard warriors roar
and I respond, always in lower case.
I try for calm as my heart rate soars.
Why can't they see the truth?
Must they believe in News Corp?
(I understand the irony here.)
The multitudes of fools are easier to ignore.
It's the misguided, reasonable ones
who conscript me into this war
against my better judgement.
There is nobody keeping score.
Half the soldiers are pretending.
What am I even fighting for?
A hope of bringing someone over,
recruiting a mind hungry for more,
but none of us will ever defect.
The battle lines are already drawn.
One side's good and one is evil
and the only thing we know for sure
is our team is always right.

Fragmented

Yesterday was the best day and then the worst,
discovering the old city under the sun and
your face twisted with rage, your words
plucking at my heart
like a guitar string
until it snapped.

I saw it coming and I couldn't stop turning the screw,
winding, stretching, until the wire split,
recoiled and
fell apart.

Later we put the pieces together but today
I'm still fragmented.

Each time it's harder to fix and harder to tune
and takes more effort
to remember
the song.

But I will never forget.

Bicycle Race

He rides in from the west,
I head east on the train.
We meet in Greece
at the pinnacles of the monks.
After years of preparation,
after two long weeks of racing,
the moment's finally come
when he will be finished
with the sweat and the pain
and all the mental strain.
No more mountains to climb,
no more gravel to cross,
no more days of pedalling
against the icy winds,
through waves of heat:
the hardest cycle of his life
will be successfully complete.
It's a herculean feat,
an olympian achievement,
a titanic triumph, though
I hope it will be his last.
Maybe I'm too bound to earth.
I don't aspire to godly wins.
The only race I want him in
is the human kind.

The Moment

The Sun sat in the sky and laughed at us.
The sky was blue, it knew it must
We sat in the boat and laughed in the sea.
be blue as the water was blue for me,
The Wind blew hard for us, for us it filled the sail.
for me the breeze was strong, it couldn't fail,
The Boat pushed through the waves so fast for you and me.
propelling the yacht swift through the sea,
You controlled the rudder, steered the boat for me.
swift under your hand because it had to be
I balanced on a toe, held by a rope, leaned far back.
so I could know the sea's smile and know about
Everything that moment contrived to make me happy.
happiness for a moment and being free.

Little Brother

I have a friend who's five years' old.
He loves to talk to everyone.
Yesterday we went for a walk
and fell into an adventure.
When you're five, the world is alive
with mystery and wonder,
with so much to see and learn and do
and no time left for doubt.

We saw a tree, so tall and strong,
we climbed into its arms,
when a man sitting on a nearby bench
was drawn towards the child.
He came over to shake his hand
and open a door between worlds.
He spoke to us of birds and spirits,
of trees and interconnections.
He told the boy he already knew,
but only had to remember.

We followed to hear his yirdaki,
a vibration from ancient years.
We stood at the centre of his song,
as it echoed through the trees.
He gave my friend a special stone
and called him *little brother*.

The boy drank every word he said
and glowed like campfire coals.
When our time together was done,
holding the rock in his small fist,
the little one said with confidence,
"I'll see you again another time."
The man smiled as he replied,
"Probably, my brother."

Moonwalk

Fifty years ago two dudes
walked on a desolate moon
followed by millions of wide eyes,
innocent faces turned to the sky,
a world awash in hope
praying for their safety,
humans for once only human
unified by the sight
of our boys leaving home.

We thought
it was the beginning of something,
an expanding of horizons,
an end, perhaps, to petty feuds.
When the astronauts returned,
disinfected from lunar germs,
both threats and adventures
were external for a while
and Earth seemed a safe haven for all.
It couldn't last.

When aliens and space viruses
failed to materialise
familiar patterns returned.
Hate and fear fell once more
into the yard next door
Look at us now.

We forgot how to cross
the vacuum between us.
We amplify differences,
our worlds divide,
orbiting off
until we're alone and
lost in space.

Same

Do we really need an alien threat
to make us see we're on the same team?
Every person alive today
relies on this Earth to survive.
All of us know we eat what she grows,
drink her water and breathe her air.

Our tears and our sweat
are the same as her seas.
Our energy comes from her energy
and it all starts in the sun.
The carbon molecules of our cells
cycle through all living beings.

We are connected forever by our home.
We walk on her soil, hide from her storms.
We feel her breezes, watch her moon.
We count her days and years.
We all have someone we love.
We all slap mosquitoes.

When we're born we are all alike,
tiny, helpless, eyes squeezed shut,
dependent on another.
It is true we are each unique,
but we all once had a mother
and we're all destined to die.

for life on earth

Mother Earth Needs to Lie Down

Another milestone.
Another millstone
around the neck of Mother Earth,
who has become a crone before her time,
bent and sweating, smothered
by unfamiliar gases.
She gave us life- food, water, oxygen-
and we took it all, ungrateful children,
and wanted more.
We tore her open like a birthday present,
drilled under her seas, ripped through her soil,
as deep as we could get, towards her core.
We took it all, set it on fire
and wanted more.
She gave us all we asked, but it was far too much.
Now her energy is burnt and she is choking on the smoke.
Our insatiable needs may mean the death
of birds, flowers, fish and ourselves,
yet still we want more.
If there will ever be a chance
to save our Mother
it is now.

Grow

I plant a tree and watch as it
grows, too slow to see, but in no time
the years rush past and its limbs
reach beyond my house.

A red seed-pod drops to the ground
nestling in a bed of leaves until
it splits in two, as roots push down and
a tiny stem shoots greenly up.

Can the infant become a tree?
In twelve more years what could be
happening around this planet
strikes my heart with icy spikes.

Although more growing's what we need,
I'm frightened for this seedling.
An impulse comes to end its life
now before the trouble starts,

but between my fingers I feel it cling
in the earth with delicate strength
and I can't deny its right to try
to stay alive, whatever that means.

Small Green World

Nowhere feels like home to me
more than my tiny garden.
I watch it all meticulously.
I listen to each plant.
So slowly it grows
that only I know
it changes slightly every day.
No-one else sees the diseases,
the lovely new leaves, the buds,
the limbs stretching for the sun.
At times other eyes might admire
flashes of flowers or fruit
but all the work it took before,
hours of increasing millimetres,
resisting endless insects,
the wilting stalks and fallen twigs,
are mine alone to note.
My garden is messy and wild,
no poison in the soil,
no lawn to manicure.
It's home to worms and ants,
visiting lizards and birds,
where nothing stays the same.
It's growth and death and birth
concealed beneath the green,
hidden under the shade.

Subtle colour

Saturday and the sky is bright.
Now the grey city seems not so bad.
I ride the red lanes beside the canals,
find a patch of grass in the sun,
watch as manic humanity passes.
The air is cold, the water swirls
with lime green life.
Black and white birds chatter and dance
with a flash of midnight blue.
It's not my world but I am here
and when I take time to adjust my eyes
all the colours are too.

Pest

Oh mosquito, how I detest you.
You swarm in my face, you bite and you buzz,
still I admit I must respect you.
You keep me awake and you carry disease,
yet yours is not an easy life.
Each meal you attempt is Russian roulette.
Even before tasting blood you might
be brushed away with a tail or get
slapped flat into oblivion.
How did you beat the odds to survive
this cruelty of evolution?
For tens of millions of years you've thrived,
annoying the entire globe,
resolutely risking life each time
you employ that hateful probe.

Freedom

A new and perfect wing
Slowly stretches itself.
The sun reflects off untried feathers,
A glint in my eye.

Warmed by dawn, the wing summons strength
And gracefully, easily,
A bird ascends,
Disappearing in the limitless blue.

rest

snake sleeping in sun
coiled, heedless of screaming birds
nothing to fear now

3 birds

kookaburra call me
swoop sudden in blue
perch low, look back
big eyes not laughing
feather my heart

cockatoo missiles
empty pine cones
drop and screech
tease claw to beak
open crestful joy

currawong hop
devil yellow gaze
turn to heaven
notes take flight
song clear as truth

Moonlight Lure

When the moon lights the way
across the sea, I want to follow,
swim to the horizon,
find the end of the world
where the water licks the sky
with no dirt in between,
no concrete or steel,
no plastic,
only cool waves, salt air,
ocean creatures,
warm moon magic
and infinity illuminated by stars,
but I know that place exists
only inside my head
and there is nowhere left
to escape this mess
so instead of swimming,
I must stay here,
stuck in reality,
cast away on this shore,
compelled to keep trying
to make it right.

The Edge of Reality

It's a miracle to find a hidden place
where no-one goes, which no-one knows,
but birds, fish, lizards, snakes
and wallabies.

It seems surreal in this unreal world
where reality's not what lives and breathes
but whatever can be imagined
by humans.

It's the fictions we create and share
which occupy all our space and time
but can threaten the viability
of actual life.

It takes so much to maintain the myths
when the material world is crumbling,
but money, nations and gods
are only fantasy.

It's microbes, plants and animals
which exist with us now on this planet,
but will be pushed to the edge of reality
by an illusion.

Dry

The dams are draining dangerously.
The creeks are sticks and stones.
The ground is brown and brittle.
The leaves die one by one.
The grass is just a memory.
The insects have all gone.
The wallabies are hungry.
The cows are skin and bone.
The bats are falling from the trees.
The koalas are nearly done.
The forest is a tinderbox.
The farmers feel alone.
The fear of fire is everywhere.
The water is trucked in.
The clouds form and blow away again.
The drought goes on and on.

World on Fire

The world is on fire this week.
From thick orange skies in the north,
I drive past smouldering black trunks,
around fallen branches glowing red on the ground,
overtaken by screaming fire trucks,
through blasting winds and searing heat
for fifteen hundred kilometres,
half the country choking in smoke,
burning eyes, itchy throat,
aching for green, yearning for rain.
Is it the future I see in these flames?
Is this hazy horizon all we have?
Do we let the arsonists win?
No. It's time to remove the fuel.
It's time to fight the fire.

Fire Plan

Ash has settled over my mind,
blocking out the light,
choking the air,
smothering the sound of my screams.

This sadness is not my own
but my heart doesn't know that;
she has taken it in
to feed it with my blood.

I cannot see the flames from here
but I'm lost in the haze.
My skin won't get burned
but I could die from smoke inhalation.

Tomorrow, they say,
it's going to get worse.
The fire will transform life into grey flakes
which disintegrate in the wind

and there's nothing I can do.

Waiting for the Storm

So there's a cyclone
spinning off the coast.
While we wait to see
if it's headed west
or north or south,
the trees moan and shake
like women dragged on the dance floor
against their will.
Branches break and drop
with shocking violence.
Leaves fly up
instead of down,
soar through windows
and scatter over tiles.
The ocean roars
twice as loud as usual,
but there's no rain yet.
The tide will be high
and floods could come,
waves may eat the beach,
or maybe not.
It might be fine
and all blow over.
Nobody knows
which way it will go
and so we wait,
listen to the sea scream
and watch the sad dance
of unwilling trees.

Reprieve

It's happening.
It's finally raining,
after the grass has gone,
after the creeks have retreated,
after the forest fires have finished,
water, too late, drains from the clouds,
streaming down off brown-tipped leaves,
dripping and splashing from dusty soil,
steaming up from molten bitumen,
releasing heat back into the sky,
to bring us in from the brink,
to soak the thirsty earth
with sweet relief.

Sun shower

Raindrops flash like mirrors
in the afternoon light.
Warm and fat,
they bounce, reflect again
and splash into shadows.
I look for the sun and swivel to see
the centre of the rainbow
emerge through clouds,
disperse the spectrum,
refract across the sky.
It curves to Earth
in a miracle of physics.
A golden glow drips over all
like sweet amnesia.
This could be
another place, another time.
I could be
anywhere, anyone.
I could be
with you, watching the rain
under the sun.

Blue Space

there is a blue space in my mind
where the ocean ebbs and flows

there is a blue space in my eyes
where the water meets the sky

there is a blue space in my ears
for the collapsing of the waves

there is a blue space in my mouth
to taste the briny splashes

there is a blue space in my nose
to smell the salt sea breeze

there is a blue space in my skin
washing away with the tide

there is a blue space in my heart
floating over the swell

there is a blue space that changes
every day and every night

there is a blue space we don't know,
the place where life began.

for life itself

Questions

How is a rock not a tree?
What's the difference between being and living?
Why did molecules become cells?
When did life first happen?
Where do chromosomes come from?
Is it growth which makes life?
Reproduction?
Death?
Who decides?
Because islands, for example, can grow,
break off into new ones
or sink under the waves and dissolve.
Are islands alive?
Are planets and suns?
Is sentient life so special or
is all life precious or is it just
an endless cycle
which just is?

Dissolution

How to solve a question when
everything's dissolving?
The problem is insolvent.
There's no salvation, no solution.
There is no absolution.
There's absolutely no absolute.
Perception's all there is.
There is no 'is'.
Nothing's completely false or true,
not even this.
Is it a test?
We can never know for sure.
We cannot know what we don't know.
We can never know what's next.
We can only guess.
We can make our cleverest estimate
based on available evidence
and hope for the best.

Water is Life

Three atoms float up to the sky,
two little hydrogen and an oxygen,
linked by a special bond.
When the air cools, they condense as one,
releasing heat in a liquid ooze,
to huddle with others inside a cloud.
As each molecule joins and transforms
its energy flows into the wind.
When the cloud grows heavy, attracting more,
a droplet detaches and descends to the ground.

Three atoms fall fast through the air,
dragged by the force of gravity
to splash into a deep, brown creek
where the water is warmer and slow,
gliding gently towards the ocean,
but before they find salt to dissolve
they are suddenly scooped by a beak,
poured down a throat, into a stomach
and absorbed in the blood of a bird.

Three atoms confined to a cell
as the temperature and altitude rises,
they pump through vessels and fly for miles
around the body and across the world
to be deposited, after many months,
in a place of quiet white.

Here the molecule stops moving,
locks with others around it,
magnetically forming a crystal
still, solid and cold.

Three atoms stay trapped in the ice
waiting for that summer day,
when the sun is finally strong enough
for them to use its energy
to break from the rest and melt away,
still joined but free to move
and drip back in the sea.

Three atoms are swept in currents,
pulled in tides and crashed in waves,
sucked into seaweed, consumed by fish,
released again to drift to the surface
until they find the heat once more
to sever the bonds, the three alone
to float away as vapour.

Three atoms connect our planet,
dancing through everyone of us,
transferring energy,
so elegant and necessary.
Nothing is more precious,
one molecule for life.

Sudden Death and the Sea

I am slammed by the shock of an unexpected death and I need to be by the sea. It is not the first time. When the world inside my head is shaken loose and set adrift, I know the ocean will still be there.

The waves roll in and roll out as they always do, never the same but never ceasing. The roar soothes my ears, so constant I don't hear it and loud enough to drown my thoughts.

There is death out there too, under the surface, beneath the smooth horizon. While the sea has plenty of problems of its own, it seems too vast to be defeated. Through wild winds and hot currents and glassy patches, through green and blue and grey, it keeps moving, it keeps cycling. It's everywhere and it always has somewhere to go.

We came from the sea and maybe one day that's where we'll return. Maybe we are not meant for this life on dry land. There are too many choices and too much free will. Look where it gets us.

Maybe the sea is where we should be, surrendering control to the flow of the tides. Maybe the ocean's our home, in the end. Until then I'll remember to walk on the beach, whenever this land is too much, whenever the ground is too hard.

Waves

We ride the waves, we surf the waves,
ocean waves, waves of emotion,
waves of sound and light.
We are submerged, we re-emerge,
we surge ahead and then recede,
we wave hello and goodbye.
Waves sweep us up and throw us down,
carry us away and crash above us;
they take us out and bring us in.
Nothing is fixed, nothing is still;
the highs and lows will never end,
the ebb and flow is eternal.

Alive

Life itself will always be
in one form or another,
though naturally we rather like our own.
If it turns out we can't halt
our train to self-destruction,
life on Earth will clear a path
through the mess we leave behind
for a hundred million years or so
until the sun destroys it.

If life is energy there'll always be
one star or another
burning and converting gas
out in the universe.
If life is more it will surely
re-create itself because
that's what it's all about.
Life is strong. Life will adapt.
Life knows how to live.

This is not a call to drop
our instinct for survival.
I will never stop the fight
for my beloved planet.
It's just a note to self to say
be strong against despair.
Even if humanity's lost,
life will find a way.

In

In the leaving is the arriving.
In the flight is the landing.
In the joy of today
is the emptiness tomorrow.
In the darkest thought
is the key to peace.
In life is death. In death is life.
In the desperation to have
is the certainty of loss.
In desiring nothing is everything gained.
In wanting is wanting. In wanting is wanting.
In the progress of civilisation
is the destruction of the world.
In the destruction of the world
is the creation of the fight to save it.
In the fight is love.
In love is pain.
In pain is hope.
In hope, despair.
In every lie is a truth.
In all truth is a lie.
In the circle is the beginning, is the end.
In the spinning infinite there
is no escape.

Spinning

When I close my eyes an orange ring burns in the black,
an afterglow of the sun beyond my eyelids or
electricity in my retinas,
a circle of time inside my brain
where birth and death are spinning, holding hands.

While absorbed in little things with minor variations,
reflections of epic dramas in family barbecues or
repetitive inner voices,
this minute is sucked out into space
where energy and matter are dancing, without end.

Wildlife

The world is wild. It can't be tamed.
Meaning is a mystery.
Let it go and watch it flow
from present into history.

As you draw a perfect square
fate may nudge your elbow.
Do your best and get some rest.
Let the pattern follow.

The rains will fall, the winds will blow,
the stars will shine at night.
Life will be and you will see
the darkness and the light.

Fish will jump and waves will crash.
never knowing why.
If you try to reach the sky
you might fall or fly.

Whether

When a hundred years go by,
whether we live or die,
whether we smile or cry,
whether we quit or try,
will it matter?

Will the weather be hot
whether we fight or not?
Should we accept our lot,
that this is the best we've got
and it isn't enough?

Whether we love or hate,
is it already too late?
Have we missed the date?
Should we lie down and wait
for the end to come?

Because the air doesn't care
if we hope or despair,
how much we can bear,
or whether we're there
to defend it.

Still I run from the night,
believing it's right,
keep the sun in my sight,
and dream that life might
somehow prevail.

Remember the Sun

When the rains come, remember the sun
still burns behind the clouds
waiting for its time to shine.

Wherever you walk, whether it's night or day,
the solar fire is alight
somewhere in space.

Whoever you are, whatever you've done,
after the darkness has passed
you will see the sunrise.

However lost you are, in the fog or the smog,
just sit for a while
until the sun lights the way.

No matter what happens, if the world still turns
and spins round the sun,
there'll be another day.

fight for life

Choices

Forests burn; we set them on fire.
The Arctic melts; we liquify it.
The ocean warms; we heat the water.
Reefs die; we kill the coral.
Glaciers disappear; we steal the ice.
Species go extinct; we destroy them.
Islands submerge; we drown them.
People will go hungry; we'll starve ourselves,
but it doesn't have to be this way.

Things could be different; we could change.
It would take some disruption; we could be brave.
The system could help us; it could work for all.
Everything is connected; we could be together.
The Earth's all we have; we could protect it.
Life is the priority; we could wake up.
Greed will consume us; we could love instead.

Longing for a Leader

Lead me, Jacinda.
Lead me away from the self-absorbed men,
from the grey-haired child in charge of my country
and that orange toddler over there.
Lead me with your sane words, your kind voice,
your clear vision of a better world.
Lead me towards the light
and I promise will follow.

Why can't we have nice things?
Where is our wise woman?
When will we grow up?
Sure, egg-boy was funny, but we need something more.
Without a leader I guess we have no choice;
the people will have to rise.

The Kids of Today

How is it for you to be to be young right now?
To be freer than we've ever been
and yet to know the certainty
that the world will never be the same,
summer and winter will surely change,
one by one disasters will come,
the seas will rise, the coasts retreat,
polar ice will melt away,
so you resist, you fight for your lives
with brave hearts and fear in your eyes
but you know you've been betrayed
by the fathers and the mothers
who didn't care enough to see
the legacy they created.

Like a snowball tumbling down a hill,
it grows and gathers speed,
crushing creatures in its path
while we run behind.
If there's anyone who can stop it rolling
before it forms an avalanche
it'll be you, the abandoned kids,
with your fast legs, your energy,
your uninhibited minds,
and your fierce will to survive.

Disrupt

No-one likes disruption but
this train has jumped the track
and is headed for a collision.

Someone has to wake the driver,
divert the course
or pull the brakes
before it's too late.

Time is short to make the switch
and there will be disturbance, sure,
but it will be nothing like
the chaos guaranteed
if we continue down this route.

Nobody wants to be the one
to risk a ticket,
to turn the heads of obedient passengers,
to rise from the seat,
to run down the aisle,
to bang on the door,
to yell for attention,
but this is what we must do
to avert certain disaster.

Why are you making me late?

Why?
Because this is our final chance.
If everything doesn't turn around right now
it will be too late.
If it's not big, bold and uncomfortable
we might as well stay home.
We may as well let go,
head blindly into oblivion,
relax and watch tv,
but we can't.

Not yet.
We can't give up on this world.
It is our only home.
This magnificent web of life
deserves our sacrifice.
It deserves our tears and sweat.
We'd rather be on the couch
blocking our ears to the truth.
It's not easy to fight for survival
but what else can you do?

When

What happens in the exact moment the tide turns?
When receding waves reverse to surge upon the shore?
When power shifts?
When the opinions of the masses evolve?
When News Corp suddenly discovers the climate crisis?
When politicians publicly acknowledge
how cruelly we treat our refugees?
It is not an accident.
The winds of change are not haphazard.
They take many long years of fanning,
spreading the news,
talking to brick walls,
falling on deaf ears,
pulling heads from the sand,
but what happens in that moment?
How do facts reform to renew the truth?
How does reality reconcile itself with its liquid nature?
Do our fluid minds ebb and flow with the moon?
When do we cling to something solid?
We move slowly, we move in circles,
we inch forward.
We hope it's not too late.

Setback

When I thought it could be
that we'd shuffled forwards
with open eyes
towards the morning,
the election was lost,
the evidence not found
and the weekend went missing.
It slipped from our hands
so now we're forced
to start again,
again,
another beginning,
digging for hope,
it's down here somewhere;
we need the light
to escape this hole.

The only way
is to keep searching
with open eyes,
to keep trying
with new ideas,
to accept the setback
as part of the path,
to know that also
we might never get out,
but whatever occurs
we keep moving
with open eyes.

Strike

(for Greta Thunberg)

Don't listen to the scientists. No,
they may spend decades studying the data
but what do they know?

Don't listen to those who belong to the land.
After tens of millennia connected to nature
how could they understand?

Don't listen to those who grow our food.
For generations they have battled the weather
but they have been fooled.

As your ears stay stubbornly shut to all,
the one voice left that may break through
is that of the Swedish girl.

Greta's call is sharp as a knife,
cutting through ignorance, apathy and greed
in the fight for her life.

It's not their future at stake.
The politicians and CEOs have done enough.
It's time to strike.

Don't listen to the bots and liars.
Hear the child who speaks the truth:
the house is really on fire.

The Speaker

If they understood they'd be on our side,
he called.
If they were told truth instead of lies,
they'd all
heed the urgent need for change.

If they knew the danger they'd share our fear,
he said.
If they could foresee the coming years
they would
fight with us for our only home.

They've been misled, they're not to blame,
he allowed.
They've been played in a political game
which now
we need to stop before all is lost.

If we know what's happening we're forced to act,
he cried.
If we see what's real we cannot hold back
or hide
from the necessary rebellion.

When the leaders deceive, it's left to us,
he implored.
When systems fail to sustain life we must
do more.
It's time for civil resistance.

Extreme

Do you ever have a feeling
that nothing else matters?
Why do anything other
than try to avert catastrophe,
the collapse of civilisation?
I see the people live their lives
as if everything's fine
and I wonder if I'm extreme,
but then there's science.
How to ignore the reports?
How to go out to eat and enjoy the heat?
How to pretend as if it won't end,
like everyone else.
Am I in a cult?
But science,
science says act now.
Why would science lie?
Why do others deny?
Is the truth too big?
Is it all too much?
Is it really easier to delude ourselves
until it's too late?
Are we really so blind?
Are we really too weak
to survive?

Decolonise

This continent was a vast, diverse network
of forests, wetlands, rivers
and 250 nations
until James Cook declared it would be
a colony.

What's a colony?
Outpost, protectorate, dependency,
or an occupied territory,
somewhere simply stolen,
someone else's home?

When white devils came and claimed
the trees, women and lives,
in exchange for sheep, sickness and lies,
they thought they had the right.
What made them so entitled?

This land's still under attack.
Rivers dry up, forests die back,
but the old nations rise up.
Finally, we'll have to see
it's time to decolonise.

Do something

When the whole world is off the rails,
resist.
When caring is called weakness,
resist.
When slogans outweigh science,
resist.
When nature is smashed by greed,
resist.
When lives are valued in dollars,
resist.
When skin is ranked by colour,
resist.

Fight to defeat the narcissist.
Fight the endless avarice.
Stand in the way of ignorance.
Stand up against blind hate.

Defend our right for equality.
Defend all life on Earth.
Some causes are worth a struggle.
Sometimes humanity demands
a little sacrifice.

Peace on the front line

We listen to trees on the front line.
We plot the campaign.
We creep through the night
to launch our attack,
stand against the insurgent.
We train, keep watch,
remain vigilant
always,

yet our soldiers are not
young men hypnotised by glory
or daydreams of violence.
In our army, menopausal women
and teenage daughters
negotiate with students,
future politicians,
an old man or two,
but not one general.

We have come all this way
because our usual days
did not contain
the momentum needed
to win the war.

Here our actions are direct,
our bodies across the line
to stop coal in its tracks,
delay the burning,
cost them dollars,
one day here and later another,
relentless
for our tomorrow.

In camp the temperature finally drops,
a wallaby thumps,
night birds call.
Despite mental checklists,
an alarm set for three,
despite the battle,
there is peace being here,
equal and free as nowhere else,
doing all we can do
for our collective
home.

Rise

Can you feel the people rising?
Can you see the sands are shifting?
Do you hear what we're demanding?
Did you know we're reconstructing?
Or are you blinkered by your dollars,
looking backwards through the tunnel
to the way things used to be?

That time has passed to history;
the paradigm has been refreshed.
We're old but we can still adapt
to a new, improved worldview.
It will mean a clear upheaval.
There will be loss of certainty,
but if we don't create the changes
they will happen anyway
in a way we'll all regret.
Step back to see the bigger picture:
life on Earth is paramount.
To preserve our existence here
we'll do whatever it takes.

This morning the sky is clear

Today I choose to hope.
I will see the young people striving to make things better
and those kind elders who haven't quit.
I will feel the autumn sun on my skin
and smell the ocean breeze.
I will hear the morning birds fill the air
and drink my coffee.
I will say to myself *it always was
and always will be*
and believe the words.
I will know we are doing our best,
some days we try harder than others,
and sometimes we rest,
but we will never give up.

for life

we keep trying, we keep trying
even when we're failing
when we're falling
when all hope is lost
when no-one cares
we push the rock up the hill
we keep trying to do what's right
because it's right
because not to fight
to accept it's over
is too much to bear
the stakes are high
the stakes are life
we go down kicking
we go down screaming
we go down burning
we won't let go
for the love of air
the love of water
the love of Earth
for life

*Thanks to the Earth for sustaining life for me
and all I love.*

www.ingramcontent.com/pod-product-compliance
Lightning Source LLC
Chambersburg PA
CBHW020233120726

47903CB00008B/2658